HACK YOUR OWN SUCCESS!

Birister Sharma

Copyright © 2022 Birister Sharma

All Rights Reserved.

Dedicated to my loving wife....

Pallabi Devi Sharma

I surrendered to you, O my
Lord......

"Om Namah Shivaya"

Table of Contents

One Word..1

1. Think big...4

2. Never give up Your Dreams.................. 10

3. Grow your inner strength 16

4. Do now!.. 22

5. Have a plan 26

6. Execute your plan................................... 31

7. Develop your self-confidence.................... 36

8. Follow your conscience............................. 41

9. Believe in yourself................................... 46

10. Keep your high spirit!............................. 50

About the author.. 53

One Word

Who is the maker of your life? Of course, you! Who is the builder of your life? Of course, you! Who can guide you in your life? Of course, you! Who can lead you in your life? Of course, you! Who can make you successful in your life? Of course, you! Who is responsible for your success and failure? Of course, you! Can you hack your success? Yes, of course, you can!

As a matter of fact, you are the maker of your own life; you are the builder of your own life. You can guide as well as lead your own life. You can make yourself successful in your life. You are also responsible for your own success and failure. And you can hack your own success as well.

However, sometimes many of you forget these actual facts and wander in your life aimlessly and purposelessly, looking for your joy, happiness, success, prosperity, peace, and tranquility elsewhere. Your joy, happiness, success, prosperity, peace, and tranquility are always within you. You just need to look inside yourself. Always remember that you are born in this world only to become successful in your life, not to become a failure and a loser.

Follow the mantras below for your success:

- Think Big

- Never give up on your dreams

- Grow your inner strength

- Do it now!

- Have a plan

- Execute your plan

- Develop your self-confidence

- Follow your conscience

- Believe in yourself

- Keep your spirits high!

꜔***꜔

"It takes the same energy to think small as it does to think big. So dream big and think bigger."

---Daymond John

3

1. Think big

"Believe big. The size of your success is determined by the size of your belief. Think little goals and expect little achievements."

---David J. Schwartz

There were two men, Suraj and Ravi. Both of them belonged to poor families. Suraj always thought of big things. He was a dreamer and ambitious. He always wanted to do something great in his life. He always wanted to achieve something special. He wanted to change his life. He didn't want to remain poor forever. He wanted to become a rich and successful man. Hence, he started working hard. He invested more quality time in himself. He started looking for all the possibilities to make himself a rich and successful man. He discovered his own strong and weak points. He started polishing his talents and skills so that he could reach his desired goal. He transformed himself in every possible manner. He focused only on his goal. He has given up all the bad habits that would distract him from his goal. He developed his personality and transformed himself into a man of determination and high spirit. He worked hard and persevered. He believed in himself. He became self-confident and self-reliant. He ultimately discovered his own destiny, and after working for five years, he became a rich and successful man.

On the other hand, Ravi always thought of himself as a poor and unfortunate man. He didn't believe in thinking big things. He had no big dreams or ambitions. He had no goals in his life. He only blamed his parents and his stars for his pitiable condition. He had a mindset of weakness and negativity. He always thought that he couldn't achieve anything in his life. He started wasting his valuable time on purposeless deeds. He had bad habits. He thought that he was not a blessed one, so he had no talents or skills. He remained idle. He only worked for his daily needs. He was not interested in exploring anything in his life. He remained unaware of his tremendous potential. He didn't want to change his life. He liked his poor and mediocre life. He thought that only the sons and daughters of rich people would become rich, prosperous, and successful. He had self-doubts and negative attitudes. He didn't believe in hard work, perseverance, self-belief, self-confidence, and self-reliance. Eventually, he lived a deprived life, and one day he breathed his last.

This story signifies that you should always think of big things in your life, as only thinking big will help you excel in your life.

The Big Thinker:

- He is a dreamer and ambitious.

- He discovers his own destiny.

- He believes in himself.

- He is confident.

- He is self-reliant.

- He knows his own strengths and weaknesses.

- He polishes his talents and skills.

- He can improve himself every day.

- He learns new things every day.

- He never quits.

- He is a busy man.

- He is focused on his goals.

- He has a positive attitude.

- He has high determination and enthusiasm.

- He has a hunger for success.

The Low Thinker:

- He has no dreams or ambitions.

- He doesn't know his own destiny.

- He has self-doubt.

- He is confused and puzzled.

- He always depends on others.

- He is weak and timid.

- He is unaware of his own talents and skills.

- He doesn't learn anything.

- He has a lack of knowledge and wisdom.

- He is a quitter.

- He is idle.

- He has no goals.

- He has a negative attitude.

- He is directionless.

- He has no purpose in his life.

How could you think big in your life?

- Clarify your goals and ambitions.

- Believe in yourself.

- Be confident.

- Be self-reliant.

- Figure out your own strengths and weaknesses.

- Polish your talents and skills.

- Improve yourself every day.

- Learn something new every day.

- Never give up anything without a fight.

- Keep yourself busy with your own work.

- Always stay focused on your goal.

- Always maintain a positive attitude.

- Be determined in every approach.

- Keep the burning desire to succeed in your life.

"Don't let small thinking cut your life down to size. Think big, aim high, act bold. And see just how big you can blow up your life."

---Garg Keller

~***~

"Once upon a time you were a small child with big dreams that you promised you'd make real one day. Don't disappoint yourself."

---Unknown

2. Never give up Your Dreams

"Never give up on what you really want to do. The person with big dreams is more powerful than one with all the facts."

---Albert Einstein

Asha was a little girl who lived in a small village. She was a great dreamer and an ambitious girl. Asha's only dream was to run like her idol P.T. Usha. (P.T. Usha has won hundreds of gold medals in many national and international games in athletics and represented India in many international events.)

Asha worshiped her idol every day and trained herself day and night in running. She ran like the gushing wind; nobody could ever beat her in her school's running race competitions. Whenever there was a running race competition, Asha always stood in first position. Hence, her schoolmates called her by the name of her idol, P.T. Usha. She was popularly known as 'the Little P.T. Usha.' She felt delighted and proud whenever anyone called her by the name of her idol, P.T. Usha.

Time elapsed in the same fashion. When Asha completed her higher secondary examination, she got an opportunity to participate in the National Games in the running race competition, which would be held in New Delhi. Asha was excited and thrilled to participate in the National

Games. She was accompanied by her coach and other players for the national event. She was traveling from her native place to New Delhi by train. She enjoyed every moment. She had already trained for the last six months for this great event.

However, on the way to New Delhi by train, the express train met with an accident in the middle of the journey; Asha was seriously injured. She was admitted to the nearby hospital as soon as possible. She was saved, but she lost her left leg. It was the most awful incident that happened to poor Asha. Her world was crumbling down. Her dream was burned down all of a sudden. She became crippled and lame; she had to walk with one leg. She couldn't run anymore for the rest of her life. She had to give up her lifelong dream of running like her idol P.T. Usha and playing for her country. Everything was washed away. Nothing was left in her life.

After three months, Asha was discharged from the hospital and returned to her house. But she hasn't given up her dream of running like her idol P.T. Usha. She has read somewhere that there was a competition in a running race for crippled or handicapped people. She has decided to wear an artificial leg and participate in the running race competition in the Paralympic Games. But it was not an easy road for her to pursue. She didn't give up her dream to die prematurely. She was determined and confident. She has a firm belief in her abilities and caliber. She trained herself day and night; she has completely devoted herself to her mission to participate in the running race competition in the Paralympic Games. She has spent more than five years rigorously and disciplined training herself. And after five years, her hard toil and perseverance paid off with fruitful results; she became eligible to participate in the running race competition in the Paralympic Games.

Eventually, Asha fulfilled her dream; she participated in the Paralympic Games and won gold medals for her country.

What is the moral of this story?

The moral of this story is to never give up on your dreams, no matter what happens in your life. If you believe in your dreams, you can fulfill every one of them. Nothing will stop you from achieving your dreams. You just need to believe in yourself. If you are determined to fulfill your dreams, the entire universe will make ways for you to achieve them.

"When you want something all the universe conspires in helping you to achieve it."

---Paulo Coelho

What happens when you never give up on your dreams?

• You can achieve whatever you want in your life.

• You can stand like a giant rock before every tough situation in your life.

• You can solve every problem in your life.

• You can build your own destiny.

• You can transform your own life.

• You can grow and develop yourself.

• You can build anything in your life.

• You can discover anything in your life.

• You can create anything in your life.

• You will never see failure in your life.

• You will become the master of your own success.

What happens when you give up your dreams?

• You can't achieve anything in your life.

• You can't face anything in your life.

• You can see problems in every solution.

• You will ruin your own life.

• You can't transform your own life.

• You will become handicapped in your life.

• You will always live a mediocre life.

• You can't discover anything in your life.

• You can't create anything worthwhile in your life.

• You will see failure in every opportunity.

• You will miss all the treasures of your life.

"Never give up on a dream just because of the time it will take to accomplish it. The time will pass anyway."

---Earl Nightingale

ﹹ***ﹹ

"Strength does not come from physical capacity. It comes from an indomitable will."

---Mahatma Gandhi

15

3. Grow your inner strength

"We all have an unexpected reserve of strength inside that emerges when life puts us to the test."

---Isabel Allende

There were two boys. Their names were Ravi and Kavi.

Ravi always wanted to build his inner strengths. So he started reading books on self-help, motivation, spiritualism, religions, and mythologies. Reading all these books helped him to know his inner strengths. He has devoted himself to learning his untapped inner potential. Gradually, he learned all his undiscovered potentials, such as his self-belief, self-confidence, self-reliance, self-discipline, and self-control. He became aware of his inner strengths and potential. Thereafter, he not only developed himself mentally but also developed himself physically.

He excelled in his life while facing all the ups and downs. Sometimes he has come across tough situations; sometimes he has witnessed countless failures; and sometimes he has faced the tragedies of his life. But he has never given up. He has fought back against every tough situation, every failure, and every tragedy, coming out with flying colors. He has earned name, fame, and prosperity in his life.

On the other hand, Kavi was only interested in building his physical health. He loved relishing good food and making fun and feasting. He maintained a balanced diet for his physical health. He had no interest in anything other than his physical health. As time passed, he built his physical health so strong and powerful that all the people admired him for his physical strength. However, he did not concern himself with his mental strength. He had a wrong notion about self-belief, self-confidence, self-reliance, self-discipline, and self-control. For him, if he built his physical health, he could do anything in his life. But as a matter of fact, life is an absolute mystery. When life starts bombarding us with various situations and circumstances, nobody can predict or speculate anything. The same thing happened to Kavi. He came across the toughest situations of his life, faced failures, and witnessed tragedies, one after another. Then what? He fell down like the leaves of a falling tree. He couldn't face the tough situations, the failures, and the tragedies of his life. He lacked self-belief, self-confidence, self-reliance, self-discipline, and self-control. He accepted his weaknesses and failures. He couldn't counteract the tough situations, the failures, and the tragedies of his life. He couldn't rescue himself. Eventually, he quit on life.

This story suggests that anything can happen in your life—good, bad, or worse. You can only counteract the tough situations, failures, and tragedies of your life with your inner strengths, such as your self-belief, self-confidence, self-reliance, self-discipline, and self-control. Therefore, you have to strengthen both your mental strengths and your physical strengths at the same time.

No magic potions
No fairy dust

No one to do it for you
Juts me, I will push you,
Show you,
How to put one determined foot in front of the other,
I am inside you.....
I'm called your inner strength.
Dig deep down and find me.

---Unknown

What are your inner strengths?

- Self-believe

- Self-confidence

- Self-reliance

- Self-discipline

- Self-control

Mental Strengths:

- Positive thinking

- Positive attitude

- Focus mindset

- Common sense (rational, reasonable)

- Instinct (Six senses)

• Conscience (sense of right and wrong)

• Foresight

Mental Weaknesses:

• Negative thinking

• Negative attitude

• Lack of focus (diverted mind)

• Lack of common sense (irrational, unreasonable)

• Lack of instinct (lack of six senses)

• Lack of conscience (sense of right and wrong)

• Lack of foresight

How can you increase your inner strengths?

• Always believe in yourself.

• Be confident in your every approach.

• Always keep a positive mindset.

• Always rely on yourself.

• Never compare yourself with others.

• Be brave.

• Discover your own potential.

• Clarify the perspective of your own life.

• Take calculated risks.

• Always keep your focus on your goal like an eagle eye.

"Go within every day and find the inner strength so that the world will not blow your candle out."

---Katherine Dunham

ഗ***ഗ

"If you are going to do something, do it now.
Tomorrow is too late."

---Pete Gross

4. Do now!

"Do it. Do it right. Do it right now."

---Spencer W. Kimball

There were two farmers living in a small village. Their names were Sukhiram and Dukhiram. Sukhiram always believed in doing his work now. He never procrastinated anything for the next day. He was a hardworking farmer. He worked the entire day in his field. He never felt tired or fatigued while working in his field. He loved and enjoyed his work. He never waited, whether for the favorable season or the unfavorable season. He always completed his farming before the end of the season. Hence, every year he would harvest handsome crops. He always remained happy and prosperous in his life.

On the other hand, Dukhiram was the complete opposite of Sukhiram. Dukhiram was a lazy farmer. He liked to enjoy his life. He always left his work for the next day, next week, next month, and next year. He postponed everything in his life. He didn't love or enjoy his work. He felt tired and fatigued while working in his field. He only waited for the favorable season. As a result, he was always lagging behind in his farming. He couldn't complete his farming on time every year. Hence, every year he would harvest poor crops. He always remained unhappy and destitute in his life.

This story signifies that you should always believe in doing things now. You shouldn't leave anything for the next day. If you want to grow and prosper in your life, then you have to act now. Don't postpone anything for the next day. If you postpone your work, then you will only postpone your own growth, progress, success, and glory.

What will happen when you do now?

• You have no time to postpone anything for the next day.

• You will enjoy your work.

• You will remain active and energetic.

• You will welcome your own growth and development.

• You will be able to build your own foundation of success.

• You will find the path to success.

• You will never complain about anything in your life.

• You will become happy and prosperous.

What will happen when you postpone everything?

• You will always postpone your own life.

• Your work will become a burden to you.

• You will remain inactive and low-spirited.

• You will welcome your own downfall and disappointments.

• You will build your own foundation of failure.

• You will find the path to failure.

• You will always complain about everything in your life.

• You will always become unhappy and poor.

"The time for action is past! Now is the time for senseless bickering!"

---Ashleigh Brilliant

᷍***᷍

"The best piece of advice that my mother gave me is to never have a plan B. She told me to stick to plan A because if you have a plan B you will inevitably fail back on it."

---Zoe Tapper

5. Have a plan

"An hour of planning can save you 10 hours of doing."

---Dale Carnegie

There were two generals of the two kingdoms.

One day, war broke out between the two kingdoms. The general of the first kingdom was a great and skilled planner. Before the war, he had made a comprehensive plan. He used all his talents, skills, and experiences in war tactics while making his war plan. He critically devised a strategy to win the war without taking any risks. He commanded his soldiers to move and fight according to the war plan. He had strictly ordered his soldiers to fight with their minds as well as with their cleverness. He urged his soldiers not to panic when they were surrounded in the middle of the battle, but to keep their cool and calm composure. He had injected the gushing wind of self-belief, self-confidence, self-reliance, self-discipline, self-control, and enthusiasm into the veins and nerves of his soldiers. He had taught the war plan to his soldiers very well. He had showered all his experiences of war upon his soldiers. He had divided his soldiers according to their capabilities and strengths. He had checked every department of his soldiers one by one. He had guided his soldiers—when to fight, when to retreat, how to fight, how to attack, how to use their strengths, and how to read the weaknesses and strengths of the enemies. He was determined to win the war easily with the help of his master plan.

However, the general of the second kingdom was not skilled or experienced in making a war plan. He was idle and poor at creating any war strategy. He had no war plan and no war tactics. He only commanded his soldiers to fight using their own skills and strengths. He didn't urge his soldiers to use their minds as well as their cleverness. He failed to examine the weaknesses and strengths of his soldiers. He didn't divide his soldiers according to their capabilities and strengths. He didn't check the departments of his soldiers. He didn't guide them. He had only ordered his soldiers to fight against the enemies. He had self-doubts and confusion. He was not determined to win the war; he had already given up.

Now, which of the two kingdoms would have a one hundred percent chance of winning the war?

Obviously, the first kingdom would have a one hundred percent chance of winning the war since the general of the first kingdom had planned well for it.

You know what? Your life is also a war, and you are the general of your own kingdom. You have to make a plan before you do anything in your life since you never know what will happen next. Therefore, you have to make a plan so that you can fight the tough situations, challenges, and circumstances of your life.

Do you have any plan for your life?

If you have a plan, then you are ready to fight in the war of your life. And if you have no plan, then be ready to face the worst consequences of your life.

With a Plan:

• You can prepare yourself.

• You can guide yourself.

• You can direct yourself in the right direction.

• You can make a blueprint of your life.

• You can get an overview of your success and failure.

• You can get a clear idea to move ahead in your life.

• You can work according to your own plan.

• You can estimate your own caliber and potential.

• You can calculate your own strengths and weaknesses.

• You can correct your own shortcomings.

Without a Plan:

• You will become unprepared.

• You will mislead yourself.

• You will always move in the wrong direction.

• You can't make any outline of your life.

• You will be overshadowed by self-doubts and confusion.

• You will get stuck.

• You can't concentrate on anything.

• You can't estimate anything.

• You will miscalculate your own strengths and weaknesses.

• You can't realize your own shortcomings.

"Have a plan. Follow the plan, and you'll be surprised how successful you can be. Most people don't have a plan. That's why it's easy to beat most folks."

---Bear Bryant

∽***∽

"A bad plan that is well executed will yield much better results than a good plan that is poorly executed."

---Otto Von Bismarck

6. Execute your plan

"Take action to build a plan, but know the real results come from taking the actions to execute it."

---Laura Lake

Once upon a time, there was a man living in a small town. His name was Chatak. He was a man of multiple talents and skills. He knew everything about the world that an ordinary man couldn't imagine or think. He was an extraordinary man. He had a profound knowledge of medicine, science, mathematics, astronomy, geography, philosophy, and business. He had thousands of great and extraordinary plans in his head that might change not only his life but also the lives of many thousands of people. He had jotted down all his great and extraordinary plans in his notebook, which he used to carry wherever he went.

However, unfortunately, he couldn't execute any of his great and extraordinary plans in his life. He couldn't gather the courage to execute his great plans. His mind was full of doubts and confusion. Whenever his subconscious mind wanted to execute his plans in practice, his conscious mind didn't allow him to execute anything. Hence, he had postponed all his plans.

Then, one fine day, he decided firmly to execute one of his extraordinary plans in his life. He was elated and thrilled. So, he started looking for his notebook frantically, but in vain. He couldn't find his notebook.

Somebody had stolen Chatak's notebook of great and extraordinary plans and executed them in his own life, earning name, fame, and wealth.

On the other hand, poor Chatak spent his entire life in a poor and mediocre state. Then, one day, he died of a broken heart, repenting his grave mistake of not executing his great and extraordinary plans.

"Average people have great plans, legends have great execution."

---Anonymous

Do you have any great and extraordinary plans in your life?

If you have any great and extraordinary plans in your life, then don't wait for anybody; don't postpone it; don't delay it; don't hesitate to execute it in your practice; just execute your plan and see the final result. Otherwise, you never know who will keep their eyes on your great and extraordinary plans. Before anybody steals your great and extraordinary plans, execute your plans straightaway in practice.

If you have plans:

• Execute your plans.

- Don't wait for anybody.

- Don't procrastinate.

- Don't let hesitation and confusion take over.

- Believe in your plans.

- Go ahead with your plans.

- Don't think about the results.

- Practice your plans.

- Don't keep your plans idle.

- Your plans are the root cause of your success and glory.

If you have plans but couldn't execute them in your life:

- It is merely a waste of time.

- It is a waste of your life.

- It just remains a daydream.

- Somebody will steal your plans.

- You won't get any benefit.

- You will cease your own growth and progress.

- You will commit a great blunder.

• You will miss your own golden opportunity.

• You will repent.

• You will become responsible for your own failure and downfall.

"Take action! An inch of movement will bring you closer to your goals than a mile of intention."

---Steve Maraboli

ᔐ***ᔐ

"It is not the mountain we conquer but ourselves."

---Sir Edmund Hillary

7. Develop your self-confidence

"Always be yourself and have faith in yourself. Do not go out and look for a successful personality and try to duplicate it."

---Bruce Lee

One day, the herd of wild elephants entered the village while grazing on the paddy crops of the villagers. They entered the village and started attacking the villagers who tried to drive them away. They not only attacked the village folks, but they also smashed the houses of the villagers. They started attacking the villagers and damaging the houses one after another. The poor village folks left their houses and ran away to save their lives. There was a house in the village where a poor old woman lived along with her dog. The poor old woman was ill and bedridden for a week; she was unaware of anything about the attacks by the wild elephants in the village.

The herd of wild elephants also entered the courtyard of the poor woman's house, but her dog was standing like a giant rock before them to save his mistress's home. The brave dog started barking at the herd of wild elephants continuously, and at the same time, he was in an attacking mood.

The herd of wild elephants tried to attack the fearless dog with their long trunks, but they couldn't reach him. He was not ready to surrender to them. The more the herd of wild elephants tried to attack him, the more he barked at them furiously and continuously.

The entire ambiance was echoing with the loud and ear-deafening barking resonance of the valiant dog, as if he were warning the herd of wild elephants to run away from his territory. The same scene went on for more than an hour. Eventually, the herd of wild elephants had to surrender to the brave dog.

The herd of wild elephants went away from the courtyard of the old woman, and they also left the village without further damaging the lives and properties of the villagers. This event implies that your self-confidence is more important than your size. If you have tremendous self-confidence within you, then you can defeat every tough enemy in your life. You will overcome every situation and circumstance in your life. You will always come out victorious.

How can you gain your self-confidence?

- Be fearless.

- Don't underestimate your own potential.

- Accept the challenges of your life.

- Know your own responsibilities.

- Perform your own duty with full devotion.

• Whatever you do in your life, give your heart and soul.

• Be firm in your every approach.

• Be positive.

• Keep your morale high.

• Keep your eyes on your target.

• Don't look back.

• Always move forward.

Lack of Self-confidence:

• Makes you fearful and doubtful.

• You will underestimate your own potential.

• You can't face the challenges of your life.

• You will run away from your own responsibilities.

• You will neglect your own duty.

• You will do everything half-heartedly.

• You will become weak and puzzled.

• You will develop a negative mindset.

• You will have low morale.

• You will miss your own direction in life.

- You will always look back.

- You can't move forward.

"Self-confidence is a super power. Once you start to believe in yourself. Magic starts happening."

---Anonymous

꙳***꙳

"Your conscience is the measure of the honesty of your selfishness. Listen to it carefully."

---Richard Bach

8. Follow your conscience

"Live with honor and follow your conscience."

---Benigno Aquino

Once, there were two young brothers who lived in a city. The elder brother's name was Bill, and the younger brother's name was Albert. Both brothers were ambitious and adventurous. They wanted to accomplish something great in their lives. Hence, Bill decided to choose the tough path, where there were thousands of challenges and hurdles ahead. But there was a permanent guarantee of joy, happiness, success, prosperity, peace, and tranquility after conquering all the challenges and hurdles.

As Bill set his first step on the tough path, he encountered thousands of challenges and hurdles in no time, one after another. He couldn't find time to settle down. He was overshadowed by thunderstorms; he was drowned in the tempest of the ocean; he was lost in the land of a dry desert; he was trapped in the tangled jungles; and he was chased by wild beasts and cannibals. But he couldn't give up. He was traveling on his tough path endlessly. After traveling on his tough path for many years, he eventually reached his destiny. The destiny he had been looking for for many years appeared before his eyes. He found himself in a heavenly abode where all the eternal joy, happiness, success, prosperity, peace, and tranquility were eagerly waiting for him.

However, Albert decided to choose the easy path where there were no challenges and no hurdles. Everything was easily available there. It was full of a lavish life, luxuries, and pleasure where anyone could enjoy to their heart's content. But there was no permanent guarantee of joy, happiness, success, prosperity, peace, and tranquility.

Albert was excited and thrilled when he found himself in the world of luxuries. He felt fortunate. He enjoyed his lavish and luxurious life without any concern. But unfortunately, after a few years, all his lavish and luxurious life vanished all of a sudden. He was dumfounded; he couldn't comprehend anything. In fact, he had trapped himself in a world of hell. But it was too late to realize anything. He couldn't turn back. He had already come a long way ahead. Ultimately, he had met his dead end.

In life, you have to follow your right path, even if it is full of challenges and hurdles. It is the law of this world that challenges and hurdles are inevitable. The challenges and hurdles of life are part of your existence. Without challenges and hurdles, your life is mind-numbing and tedious. It is only the challenges and hurdles of life that edify you about the true purpose and meaning of life. The challenges and hurdles of life never make you weak and ailing, but rather make you stronger and more powerful. Where there are challenges and hurdles in life, there are always hidden joy, happiness, success, prosperity, peace, and tranquility.

On the contrary, if you want an easy life, then you are just inviting your own anxieties, stresses, fatigue, and tensions. The lavish and luxurious things that are available without facing any challenges and hurdles are always temporary. These things will fade away within a few days.

Therefore, always follow your right conscience in your life so that you can relish the eternal bliss and tranquility of your life perpetually.

Your Right Conscience:

- It will always act as your true friend.

- It will always guide you to the right path.

- It will always help you discover your own destiny.

- You can realize what is right for you and what is wrong for you.

- It will always enlighten you to know your true purpose and the true meaning of your life.

- It will always lead you to the path of joy, happiness, success, prosperity, peace, and tranquility.

Your Wrong Conscience:

- It will always act as your enemy.

- It will always guide you to the wrong path.

- You will always wander and lose yourself in your life.

• You won't realize what is right for you and what is wrong for you.

• You will always remain unaware of the true purpose and true meaning of your life.

• It will always lead you to the path of sorrow, unhappiness, adversity, chaos, and discontentment.

"Never do anything against conscience even if the state demands it."

---Albert Einstein

ᔇ***ᔆ

"Nobody will believe in you unless you believe in yourself."

---Liberace

45

9. Believe in yourself

"You are what you believe yourself to be."

---Paulo Coelho

Jadav Molai Payeng is a farmer from Assam. When he was a young man, one day he witnessed many dead snakes and animals lying on the barren land by the floodwaters. He was astonished and shocked; his heart started trembling while seeing the poor beasts lying dead. There were no plants and no trees, only the wide-spreading barren land everywhere.

Jadav decided to change that barren land into a dense forest and bring back all the natural flora and fauna. It was not an easy job for him to initiate that task.

From the very next day, he started his mission of transforming that barren land into a dense forest. Every day, he took his small boat, crossed the riverbank, collected small saplings of plants and trees in his bag, and planted them in the barren land alone. He continued his great mission every day with new hope and zest. However, his family members, relatives, friends, and neighbors asked him to stop that madness. They urged him to abandon that worthless work and focus on his job so that he could look after his family.

But he was firm and determined in his mission. He believed in himself and that he would turn that barren land into a dense forest one day. He kept himself busy with his mission. Nobody could demoralize him.

In many instances, he has to face tough situations, challenges, and circumstances. Sometimes the plants and trees didn't grow and develop well; sometimes the blowing wind broke down the well-grown plants and trees and washed them away with the river water. But he didn't give up on his mission. He worked on his mission tirelessly.

Every day, he began with a new mission. He worked with his heart and soul to accomplish his mission of turning that barren land into a dense forest. He himself started making manure by natural methods; he himself brought the earthworms to restore the natural health of the barren land.

And eventually, his hard toil has paid off with productive results. He has spent more than 30 years transforming that barren land into a dense forest. He has planted 40 million trees and created a real man-made forest by transforming the barren land into a dense forest, covering an area of 550 hectares, which is known as 'Molai Kathoni.'

It is now the home of many birds, tigers, elephant herds, deer, rabbits, and a wide diversity of native and migratory species, as well as thousands of trees.

Today, Jadav Molai Payeng is known as 'The Forest Man of India.'

For his great contribution in the field of forestry and the environment, he was awarded the 'Padma Shri Award' by the Government of India in 2015.

What lessons can you gain from this real event?

• Always believe in yourself.

• Everything is possible if you believe in yourself.

• Don't listen to anyone else.

• Do what you believe in your life.

• Your self-belief is the mantra of your success.

• Don't wait for anything.

• Start now.

• You can transform everything with your own self-belief.

• If you have self-belief, then you can do anything; you can achieve everything.

• You can make a great difference in your life.

"Believe in yourself, push your limits, experience life, conquer your goals and be happy."

---Joel Brown

ᴗ***ᴗ

"Even if everything is destroyed, keep your spirit high because this will put everything into its place again!"

---Mehmet Murat ildan

10. Keep your high spirit!

"You are braver than you believe, stronger than you seem and smarter than you think."

---Unknown

The battle of Thermopylae was fought between the Persians and the Greeks in 480 B.C. The Persian invasion of Greece was resumed by King Xerxes in 480 BCE after the defeat at Marathon. The Greek army was led by the Spartan King Leonidas.

King Leonidas was a brave king; he was a great warrior and leader. He had chosen his best men for this battle. He and his 300 valiant men tried to block the Persian advance at the pass of Thermopylae, even though they knew that they couldn't defeat the mighty armies of Persia, but they fought bravely and resisted. They were not ready to retreat and surrender.

King Leonidas said to his 300 brave men, **"No retreat, no surrender. That is Spartan Law. And by Spartan law, we will stand and fight... and die. A new age has begun. An age of freedom! And all will know that 300 Spartans gave their last breath to defend it!"**

However, they were defeated despite brave resistance against irresistible odds. They had held for two days successfully, imposing heavy casualties on the Persian armies while suffering relatively light losses themselves. But after three days, they were betrayed, and the armies of the Persian king Xerxes I were able to defeat them.

Leonidas and his 300 brave men stood like a giant mountain before the mighty armies of King Xerxes and fought until the last breath of their lives. They had resisted until the end and were killed to the last man.

Leonidas and his 300 brave men are said to have refused to retreat because it was contrary to Spartan law and custom. They had accepted the flowers of arrows in their hearts for the sake of their own nation. Meanwhile, the largely Athenian Greek naval force received news of the defeat at Thermopylae and withdrew from Artemisium after a drawn battle with the Persian fleet.

Leonidas' sacrifice, along with that of his Spartan hoplites, did not prevent the Persians from moving down the Greek coast in Boeotia. In September 480 B.C., however, the Athenian navy defeated the Persians at the Battle of Salamis, after which the Persians returned home.

Leonidas and his 300 brave men had demonstrated a willingness to sacrifice themselves for the protection of the Greek region.

What lessons can you take away from this great historic event?

- Be brave.

- Don't be afraid of anything.

• Be ready to face every tough situation, challenge, and circumstance in your life.

• Never surrender.

• Be firm and determined in your own aims and objectives.

• Prepare yourself every day.

• Don't be afraid to sacrifice for your success.

• Believe in your own abilities.

• Always keep your spirits high, no matter what happens in your life.

• You can build your own destiny.

"There will come a time when you believe everything is finished, that will be the beginning."

---Louis L'Armour

〜***〜

About the author

Birister Sharma is a full time author. He is also an avid reader. He loves reading, writing, and motivation. He has penned down dozens of self-help motivational books and novels so far.

You may contact him @ birister2007@gmail.com